Restoring Muddy Creek

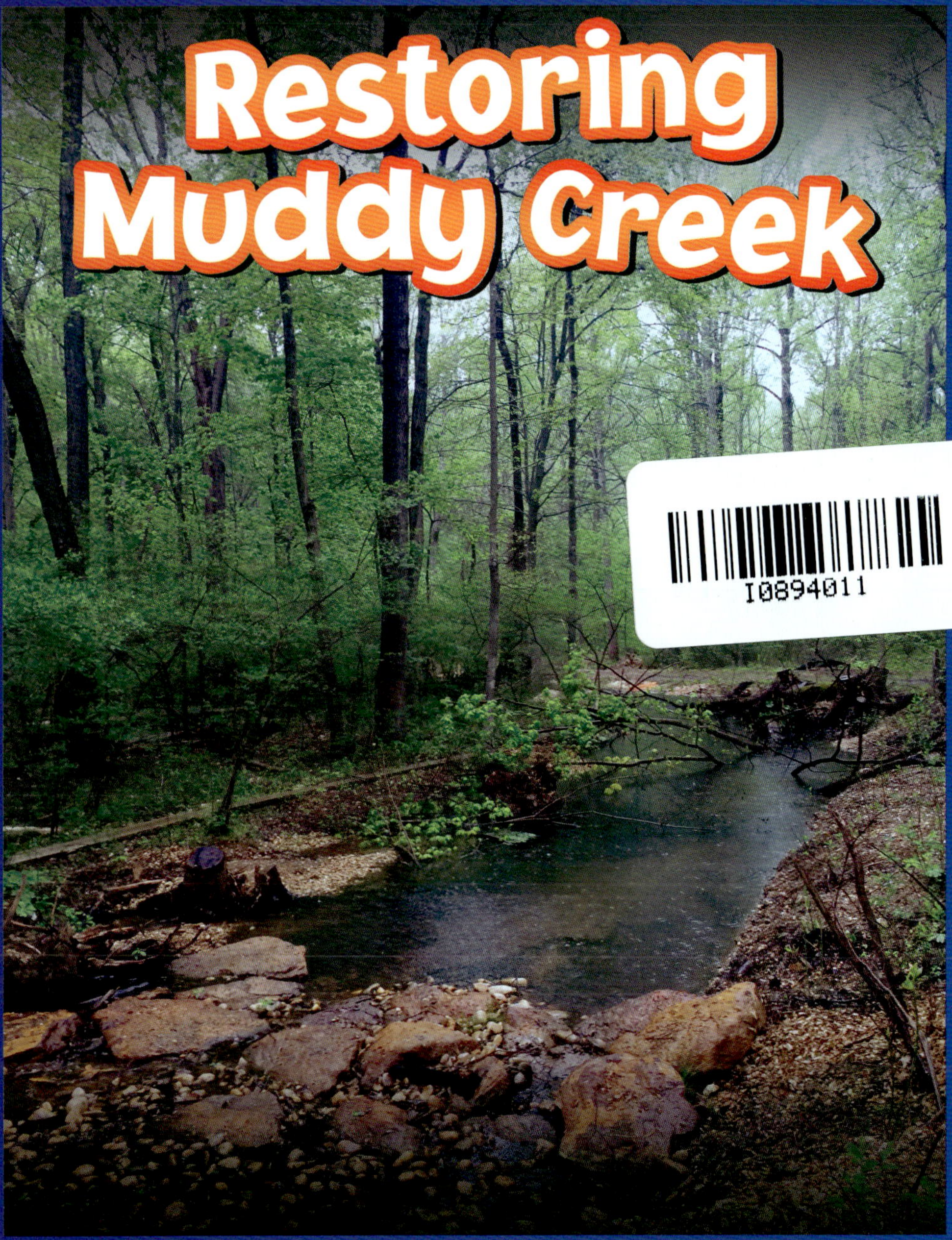

Nicole Sipe

Smithsonian

Contributing Author

Allison Duarte, M.A.

Consultants

Tamieka Grizzle, Ed.D.
K–5 STEM Lab Instructor
Harmony Leland Elementary School

Karen S. McDonald
Education Program Coordinator
Smithsonian

Publishing Credits

Rachelle Cracchiolo, M.S.Ed., *Publisher*
Conni Medina, M.A.Ed., *Managing Editor*
Diana Kenney, M.A.Ed., NBCT, *Content Director*
Véronique Bos, *Creative Director*
June Kikuchi, *Content Director*
Robin Erickson, *Art Director*
Seth Rogers, *Editor*
Mindy Duits, *Senior Graphic Designer*
Smithsonian Science Education Center

Image Credits: front cover, p.1, pp.2–3, p.5, p.11, p.12, p.13 (top), p.16 (all), p.17, p.18 (insert), p.19 (top), p.23 (bottom 3), pp.24–25, p.27 (insert) © Smithsonian; p.14 (right) Gary Neil Corbett/ SuperStock; all other images from iStock and/or Shutterstock.

Library of Congress Cataloging-in-Publication Data

Names: Sipe, Nicole, author.
Title: Restoring Muddy Creek / Nicole Sipe.
Description: Huntington Beach, CA : Teacher Created Materials, [2018] | Audience: K to grade 3. | Includes index.
Identifiers: LCCN 2017060487 (print) | LCCN 2017061785 (ebook) | ISBN 9781493869183 (e-book) | ISBN 9781493866786 (pbk.)
Subjects: LCSH: Stream restoration--Maryland--Juvenile literature. | Restoration ecology--Maryland--Juvenile literature. | Erosion--Juvenile literature.
Classification: LCC QH76.5.M3 (ebook) | LCC QH76.5.M3 S57 2018 (print) | DDC 333.91/62--dc23
LC record available at https://lccn.loc.gov/2017060487

Smithsonian

Teacher Created Materials

5301 Oceanus Drive
Huntington Beach, CA 92649-1030
www.tcmpub.com

ISBN 978-1-4938-6678-6

Printed by: 51497
Printed in: China

Table of Contents

A Unique Creek

Creeks are important to living creatures. Many kinds of fish live in them. Insects lay eggs in them. Creeks are places where frogs make homes, birds take baths, and kids play on hot summer days. Without water sources like creeks, life could not survive.

One important body of water is called Muddy Creek. It is in Edgewater, Maryland. This small creek is important because it is the site of a major makeover. For a long time, Muddy Creek was out of balance. The land around the stream was worn down. This caused the water to flow faster when it rained a lot. Fast-moving water in a small stream is harmful. Fast water destroys the homes of the animals that live in and near it. It can also carry more **pollution** and waste with it. Muddy Creek was a mess for many years, until scientists set out to restore it.

Edgewater, Maryland, USA

A scientist collects data at Muddy Creek.

Life Is But a Stream

Muddy Creek is a small stream but it has a big impact on nature. All the land on Earth is part of a **watershed**. Drop by drop, the water from rain and snow goes into the ground. It makes its way into creeks and rivers. Then, it ends up in the ocean. A change in even one small creek can affect an entire watershed.

To understand how important creeks are, think about your body. It is made up of veins and arteries that carry blood all around your body. Earth works in a similar way. But instead of veins and arteries, Earth has creeks and rivers that carry water all around the world. This water is needed by every living thing.

A river flows into the sea.

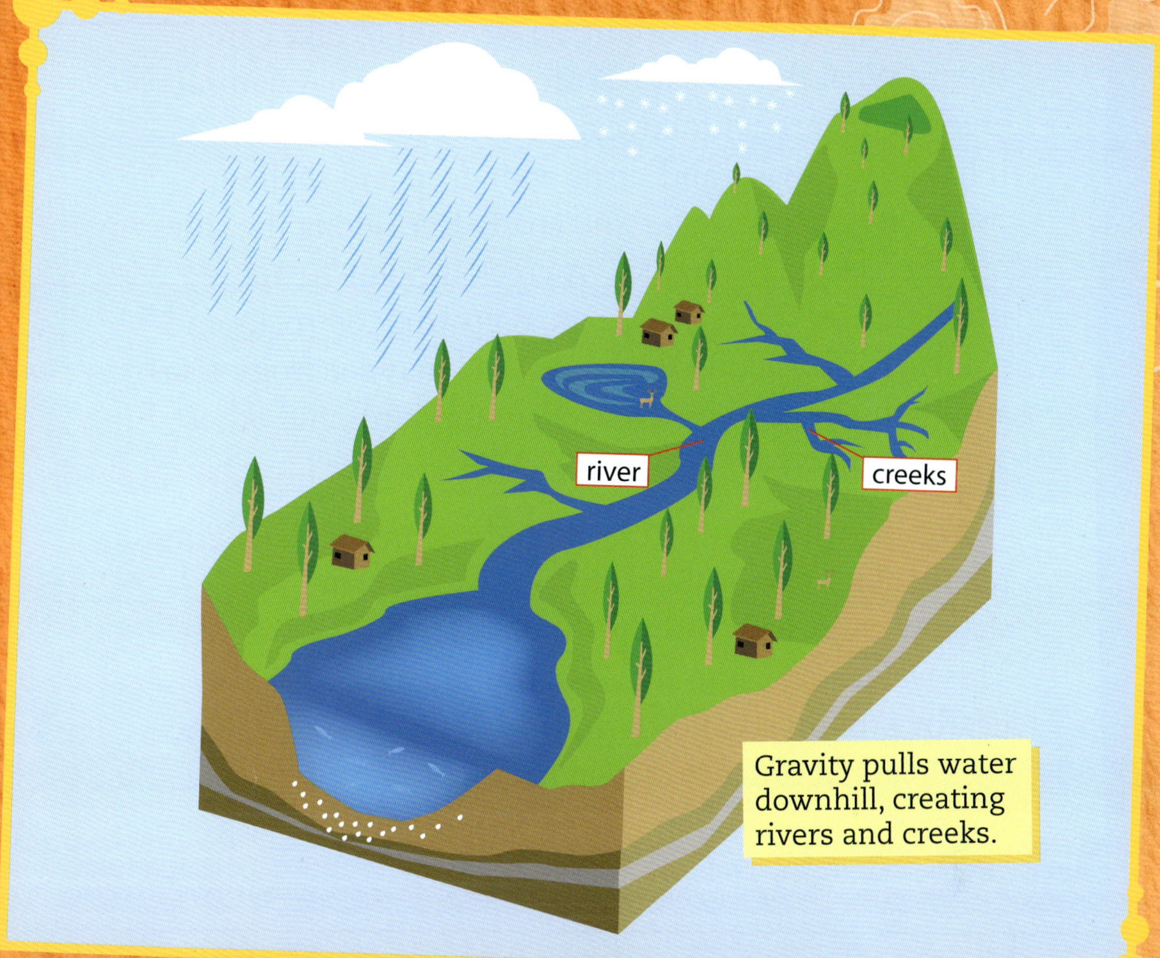

Gravity pulls water downhill, creating rivers and creeks.

SCIENCE

Pulling Water

When it rains or when snow melts, **gravity** pulls the water downhill. The land absorbs some water. The rest flows along the surface of the land. Rivers and streams are formed. They flow into larger bodies of water, such as lakes and oceans.

Waterways are important, so we want to take care of them. What does a natural creek look like? A natural creek bed does not follow a straight path. Instead, it has lots of twists and turns with deep and shallow pools. It has clear water and shady trees along the sides of the creek, called **banks**. A creek is home to many living things. You may see moss growing on rocks and plants growing along the bank. You may see frogs, fish, and flying insects. You may also spot birds and other animals at a creek.

An area with natural creeks and streams is also better prepared for floods. During heavy rain, water in a shallow creek will flow over the banks of the creek. This water soaks into the flat ground nearby. The nearby ground is called a **floodplain**. A creek needs a floodplain in order to stay in balance.

Ducks rely on creeks for food and water.

Most of Earth's surface—almost three-fourths of it—is covered in water. But only a small amount is usable by humans.

Balancing Act

Muddy Creek started out in balance. Over time, this changed. It didn't happen all at once. It took many years. Little by little, the creek bed wore down. It dropped 3 meters (10 feet) below the floodplain. When heavy rains fell, it didn't flow over the banks and onto the floodplain. Instead, it just made the water flow faster, which made the creek bed wear down even more. Muddy Creek was out of balance.

A creek without a floodplain cannot stay in balance. This flat land is important. It is even more important when there is a storm. Without a floodplain, extra water rushes through the stream very quickly. Fast water carries **sediment** with it. It makes a creek wear down quickly. It removes important minerals from the soil.

Seasonal flooding can be helpful. Floods add nutrients to the soil and refill underground water supplies.

Muddy Creek before restoration

How did Muddy Creek get so worn down? It happened because of **erosion**. Rocks, dirt, and other things in Muddy Creek became loose. Then, these things were moved by water, ice, wind, and gravity. Erosion is a natural process. It can take thousands of years. But humans can speed it up. Changing a creek in any way can affect where and how much erosion occurs.

Scientists think that Muddy Creek wore down after a **culvert** was added to it. This tunnel was built to direct the flow of the water under a nearby road. The tunnel connected the creek from one side of the road to the other. It worked for a while. But the tunnel was narrow and made the water flow very fast. This fast water made the land around Muddy Creek erode.

This section of Muddy Creek eroded 3 m (10 ft.).

TECHNOLOGY

Speeding Water

Forcing water through a narrow space makes it move faster. Garden hoses and showerheads are designed like this to speed up the flow of water.

Erosion and Stream Health

If you ever get the chance to visit a stream, take a look around you. You might notice signs of erosion. Cracks in the soil along the banks are one sign. Trees with exposed roots are another. Brown or muddy water is also a sign.

When a creek erodes, dirt is washed away from the bank. This dirt is also called sediment. A stream with a lot of sediment can hurt animals that live in the water. The dirt gets in the spaces between rocks where fish live. This makes it hard for the fish to find homes in the rocks. It also **suffocates** fish and their eggs.

When scientists **evaluate** a body of water, they often look at the living things in and around it. Insects are one type of creature they pay attention to. When the types of insects in an area change, it is a sign that the **habitat** is also changing.

dragonfly

white perch

Muddy Creek is home to more than 133 species of fish, reptiles, birds, mammals, and other creatures.

Exposed roots are a sign of erosion.

Restoring the Creek

A plan was needed to restore Muddy Creek. What could be done to help the stream? Scientists broke the project into steps. Three important things needed to happen.

First, the creek bed needed to be raised. The creek bed had eroded too much. It was too deep to let water spill over into the floodplain. To restore the creek, the creek bed needed to be closer to the floodplain.

Second, the water in the creek needed to slow down. Slower water would decrease erosion and damage to the creek in the future.

Third, the floodplain needed to be restored. Many of the water-loving plants that once lived on the banks of Muddy Creek had died. Plants that thrived in dry soil grew in their place. Many animals that lived on the banks had to find other homes. A raised creek bed would restore the area. Plants would regrow. Animals that had left would be able to return.

Scientists collect water samples.

Workers raise Muddy Creek up to the floodplain.

Nearly 6,000 kilometers (3,700 miles) of streams across Maryland are set to be restored by the year 2025.

Raise It Up

To raise Muddy Creek, the creek needed to be filled. It was like filling a hole with dirt, except that the hole being filled was 410 m (1,350 ft.) long!

First, a small pipe was added to the creek. This pipe would let the creek flow underground during the restoration.

Next, materials were poured over the pipe and into the creek bed. Scientists selected a mixture of sand and wood chips. These kinds of materials are used for stream restorations because they are natural. They create a space for plant roots to grow. When plant roots grow in the soil, they help hold the soil in place. This helps slow erosion.

Lastly, the underground pipe was removed. Slowly, the water began to flow in its bed again. It filled the newly restored creek.

Pipes like these let scientists test water under the ground while the creek was being restored.

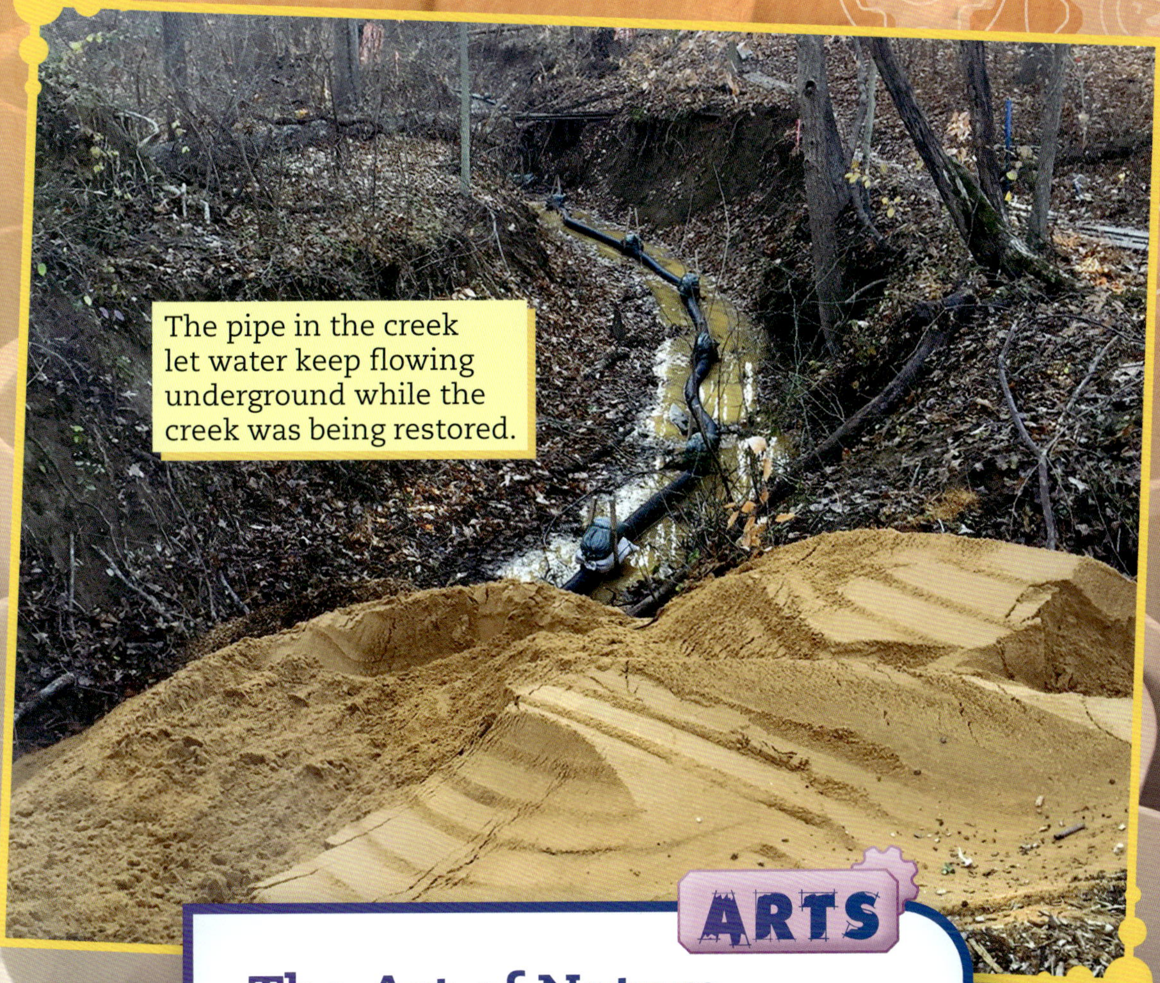

The pipe in the creek let water keep flowing underground while the creek was being restored.

ARTS

The Art of Nature

Stream restoration is a mix of science and art. The goal is to repair a damaged stream. But it must be done with respect to the landscape. Scientists do this by **mimicking** a great artist: Mother Nature. Sand, leaves, wood, and rocks help the creek without taking away from its natural beauty.

Slow It Down

The next thing to do was to slow down the water in the creek. Rocks and boulders were added to the stream in certain places. Shallow pools of water were also created all along the creek. Small dams were built out of logs and sticks. The creek was widened in places to spread out the water. All these things made Muddy Creek flow more slowly.

A slow creek is peaceful to see. But it is also important for other reasons. Fast-moving water makes a creek erode faster. A floodplain needs water to move slowly so that it has time to soak into the ground. If water is moving too fast, it will continue to flow above the ground. This washes important nutrients away from the floodplain. These nutrients are needed to keep the soil in the floodplain rich.

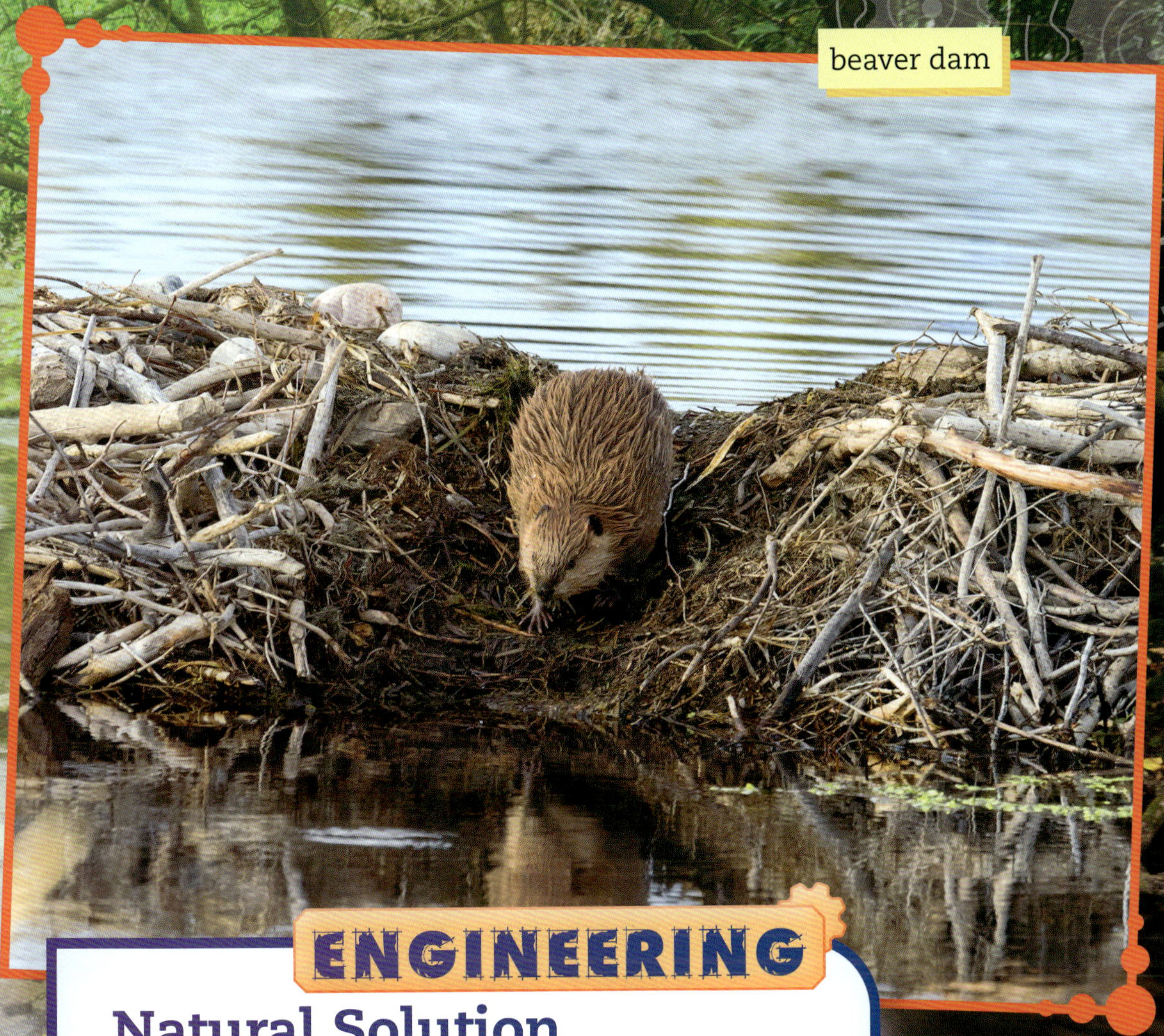

ENGINEERING

Natural Solution

In the wild, beavers are known for making dams. Beaver dams help slow the flow of water. Scientists fix streams by building structures that look very much like beaver dams. These structures are made of wood and plants, just like beavers would use. They help reconnect floodplains to their waterways.

Restored Floodplain

Muddy Creek was raised and began flowing slower. Now, the floodplain could change back. It was now mostly level with the creek. It was not 3 m (10 ft.) above the water like it once was. The floodplain could again be a habitat for native trees and plants.

Before the creek eroded, red maple trees grew along the banks. These trees grow well in wet soil. They thrived in the wet soil found next to the creek.

But then, Muddy Creek became too deep to reach the floodplain. The red maple trees were cut off from the water. Beech trees and tulip poplars grew in their place. These trees grow well in dry soil.

After Muddy Creek was restored, scientists noticed that red maple trees started growing again along the banks. The tulip poplars began to die off. These were signs that Muddy Creek was changing.

white-tailed deer

red fox

Mammals rest and look for food in floodplains. These areas are also stops for migrating birds.

red maple tree branch

before

during

after

A Success Story?

The restoration of Muddy Creek began in January 2016. By summer of the same year, the creek looked very different. It was well on its way to being restored. Muddy Creek now had flat, low banks. The wide stream had new red maples growing next to it. Insects buzzed above the gentle water. Frogs croaked from behind logs. Birds sang in the shade of the trees that lined the stream.

Muddy Creek seemed like a success story. Right? Well, not everyone would agree. Red bacteria began to grow after the creek was restored. Many parts of the creek became coated in a red film. Scientists are trying to figure out why this is happening. They also want to know if the bacteria will harm the creek's **ecosystem**. No one has answers to these questions yet.

Red bacteria grows in Muddy Creek after it was restored.

A scientist collects a sample of red bacteria from Muddy Creek.

MATHEMATICS

Seeing Red

What is making the red bacteria grow in Muddy Creek? Scientists are using math to find out. First, they collected small samples of the creek water and bacteria. Then, they tested the water multiple times. Comparing the data from the tests showed that the oxygen level dropped over time. But why? Scientists need to run more experiments to know for sure!

Restoring a creek is not simple. It is hard to tell whether the project is a success. It takes a long time to see results. Scientists know that raising a creek bed helps the flow of the water. But creek restoration is still new. It will take many years of watching Muddy Creek to find out how it reacts over time. Then, they will know whether restoring a creek is worth the time and cost in the long run.

Muddy Creek is just one of many streams that has been restored. Other projects like it are taking place all around the world. Scientists **debate** the best way to restore waterways. But everyone agrees that our waterways need attention and care.

A scientist explains the importance of creek restoration.

STEAM CHALLENGE

Define the Problem

Now that you know how erosion changes a creek, what can you do to prevent it? Your first task is to build a creek with sand and soil on a flat surface, such as a lunch tray. Then, add materials in and around the creek to reduce erosion. Which materials will work best?

Constraints: Your model can only include three of these five materials: pebbles, mulch, moss, small bags of sand, and cardboard squares.

Criteria: Your design must decrease the amount of sediment washed away by $\frac{1}{2}$ liter (about 2 cups) of water poured through the creek.

1 Research and Brainstorm

What makes water in a creek change speed? How does erosion change a creek? What did scientists do to restore Muddy Creek?

2 Design and Build

Sketch your creek. Include where you will place the materials. Place the creek in a large box. Lift one side of the box 8 centimeters (3 inches). Pour water into the creek and collect the water and sediment as it flows out. Measure how much sediment is washed away. Add the materials in and around the creek.

3 Test and Improve

Pour water through the creek again with the materials in place. Is there more or less sediment? Was your design successful? How can you improve it? Modify the placement of the materials, and try again.

4 Reflect and Share

Did your design reduce erosion? How do you know? Compare your model to other models in the class. What can you learn from other models?

Glossary

banks—the ground that is at the edge of a river, stream, or creek

culvert—a pipe or drain that lets water flow under a road or railroad

debate—to express different opinions about something

ecosystem—community of living and nonliving things in a particular environment

erosion—movement of weathered rock and sediment

evaluate—to judge the value of something in a thoughtful way

floodplain—an area of low, flat land along a body of water that may flood

gravity—a force that acts between objects, pulling one toward the other

habitat—the natural home of an animal, plant, or other organism

mimicking—to imitate closely

native—born in a certain place

pollution—substances that make land, water, and air dirty and not safe to use

sediment—very small pieces of rock, such as sand, soil, and dust, that settle to the bottom of a liquid

suffocates—kills someone or something by making it impossible to breathe

watershed—an area of land that drains into a common ocean, lake or river

Index

CAREER ADVICE
from Smithsonian

Do you want to help restore nature?
Here are some tips to get you started.

"Stream scientists start out in school just like you. To become a stream scientist, study math and science. Visit parks with streams like Muddy Creek. Explore the creeks by turning over rocks to look for aquatic insects, but be sure to roll them back, too!" ***—Karen McDonald, Smithsonian Environmental Research Center***

"To understand ecosystems, you need to look at the complex interactions of living things on Earth. These interactions make ecosystems work. Study subjects such as ecology, biology, evolution, and conservation of marine organisms." ***—Emmett Duffy, Biologist***